AUDIO ACCESS INCLUDED

CHRISTMAS SONGS
FOR SOLO FINGERSTYLE GUITAR

16 Fun-to-Play Holiday Favorites Superbly Arranged in Standard Notation and Tab

Arranged by Pete Billman
Recorded by Doug Boduch

To access video, visit:
www.halleonard.com/mylibrary

Enter Code
6551-4088-6929-7980

ISBN 979-8-35010-129-4

HAL•LEONARD®

Visit Hal Leonard Online at
www.halleonard.com

World headquarters, contact:
Hal Leonard
7777 West Bluemound Road
Milwaukee, WI 53213
Email: info@halleonard.com

In Europe, contact:
Hal Leonard Europe Limited
1 Red Place
London, W1K 6PL
Email: info@halleonardeurope.com

In Australia, contact:
Hal Leonard Australia Pty. Ltd.
4 Lentara Court
Cheltenham, Victoria, 3192 Australia
Email: info@halleonard.com.au

Baby, It's Cold Outside

from the Motion Picture NEPTUNE'S DAUGHTER

By Frank Loesser

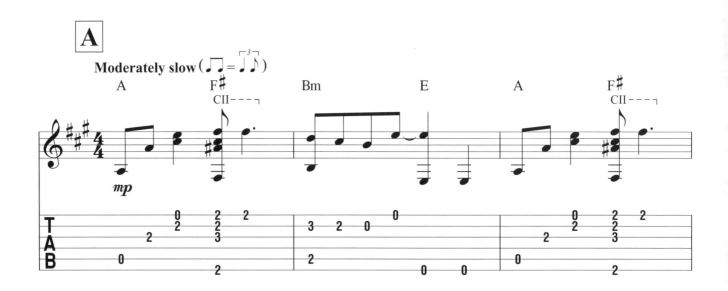

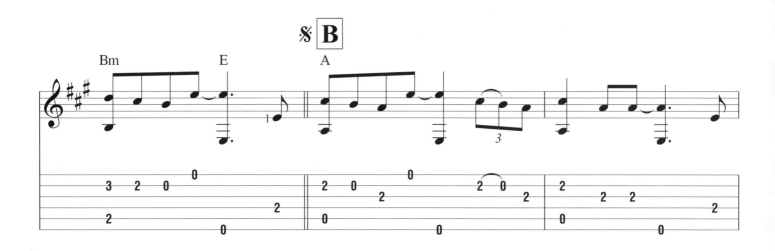

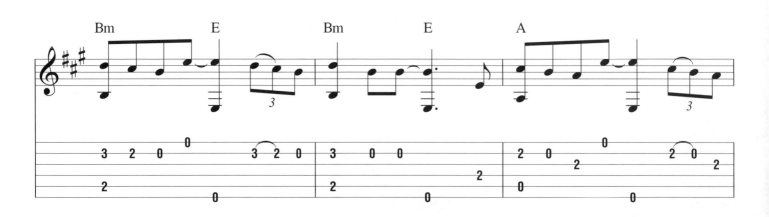

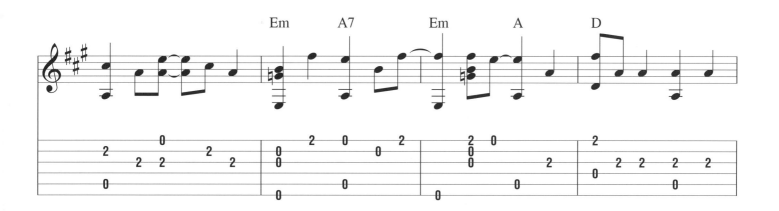

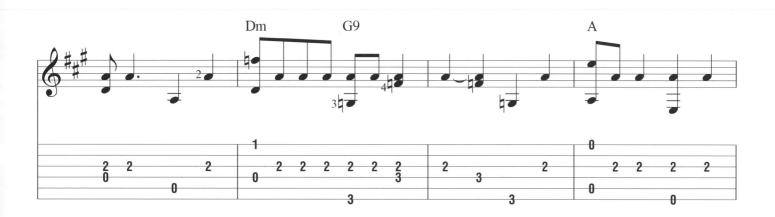

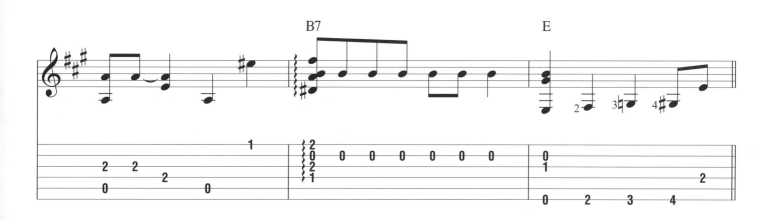

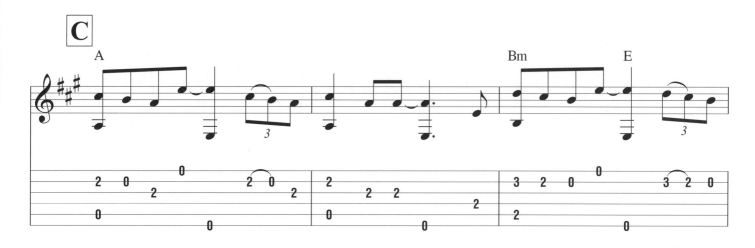

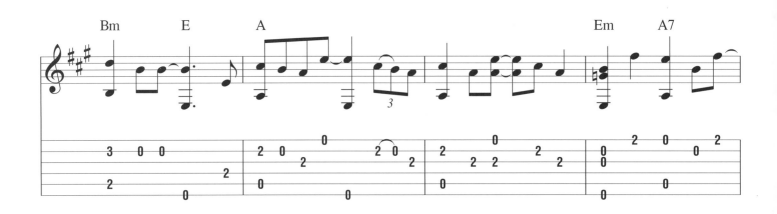

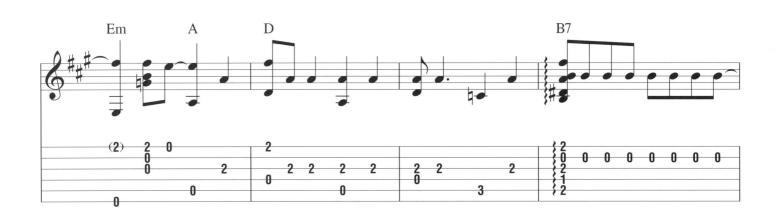

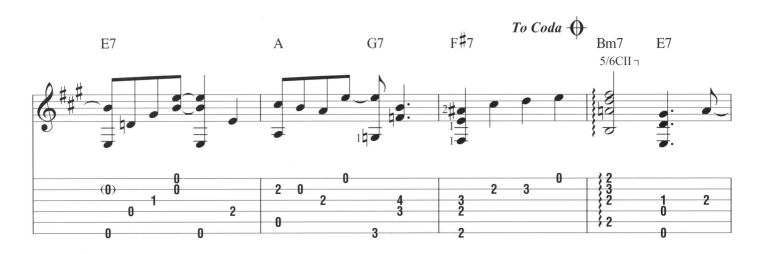

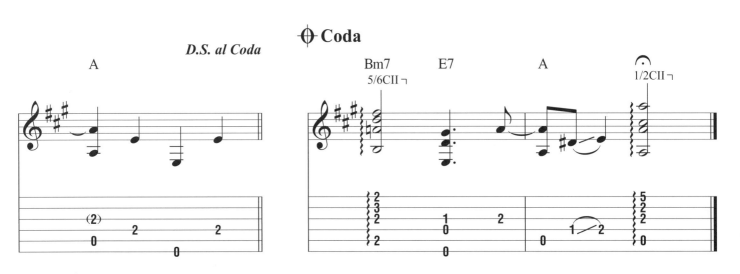

The Christmas Song
(Chestnuts Roasting on an Open Fire)

Music and Lyric by Mel Tormé and Robert Wells

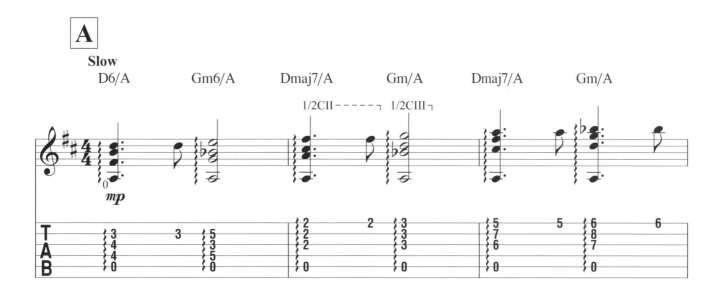

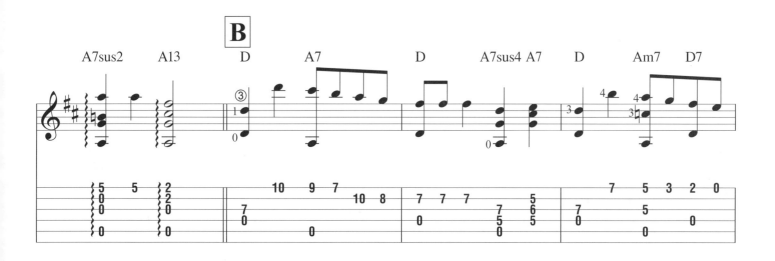

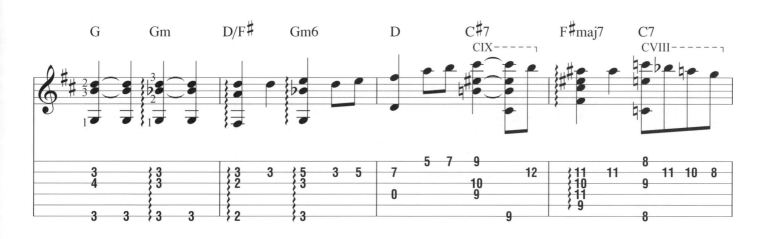

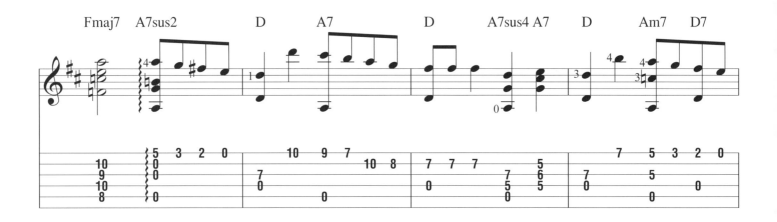

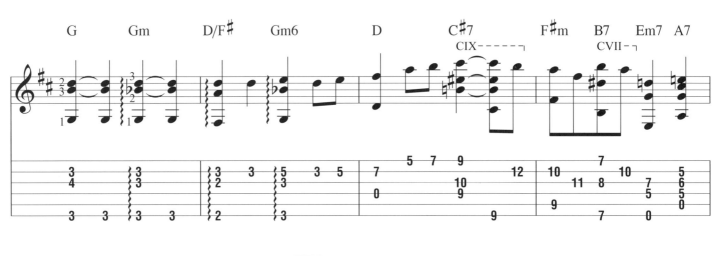

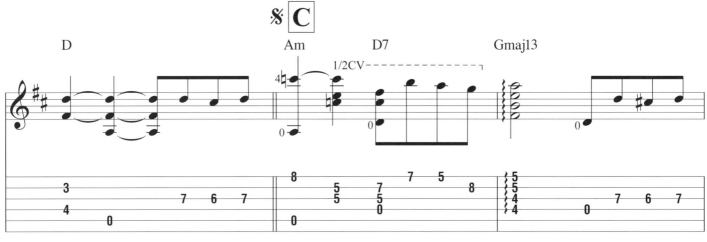

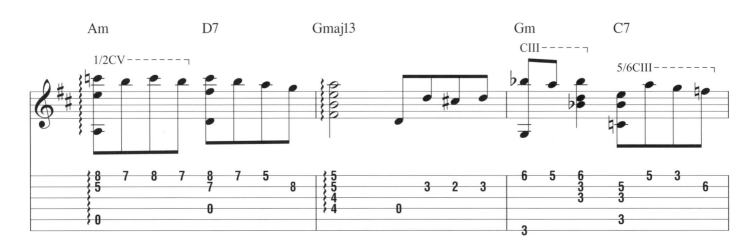

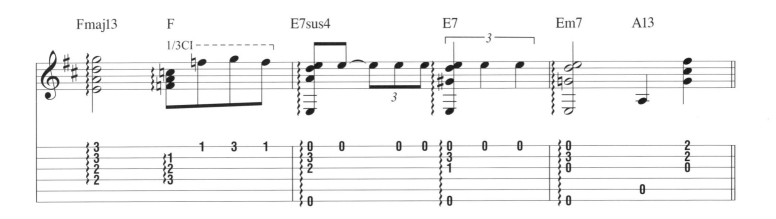

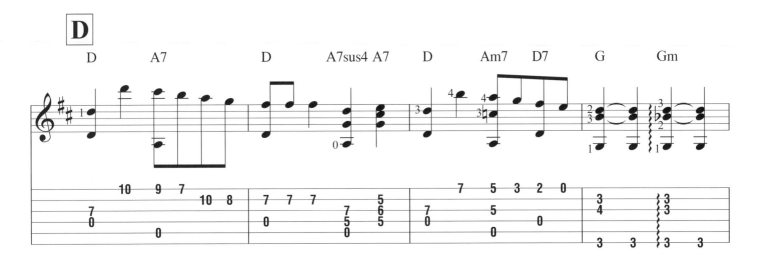

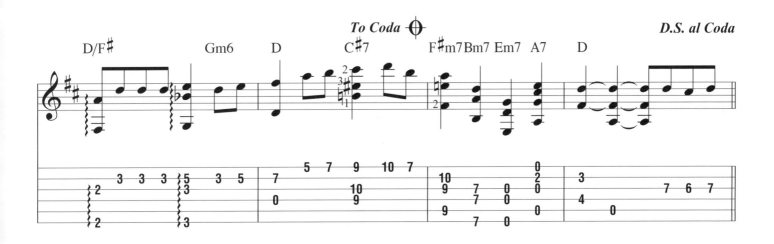

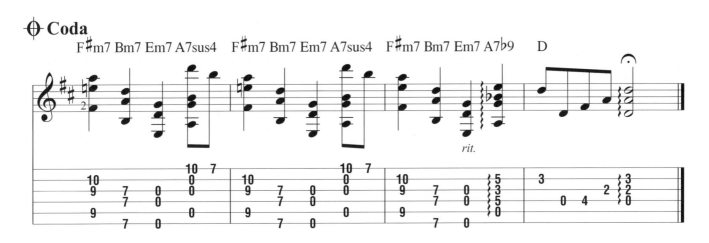

Blue Christmas

Words and Music by Billy Hayes and Jay Johnson

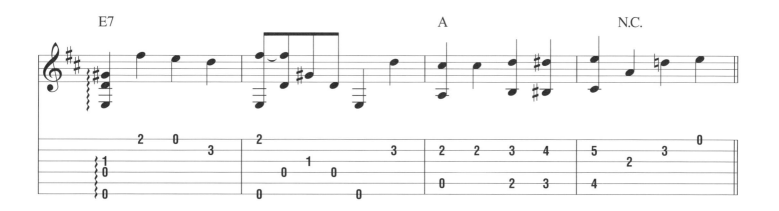

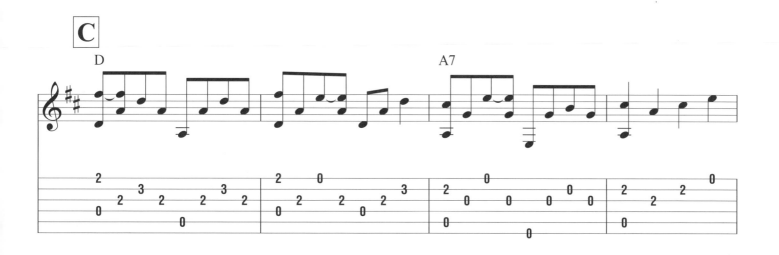

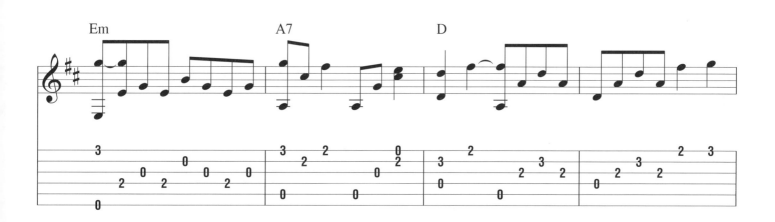

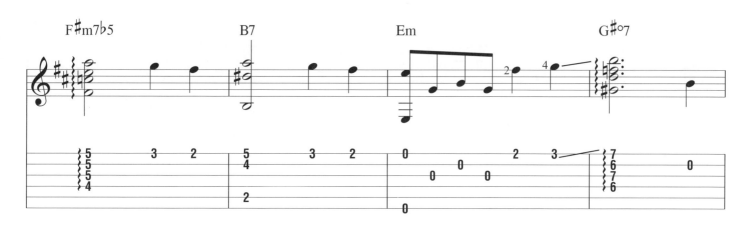

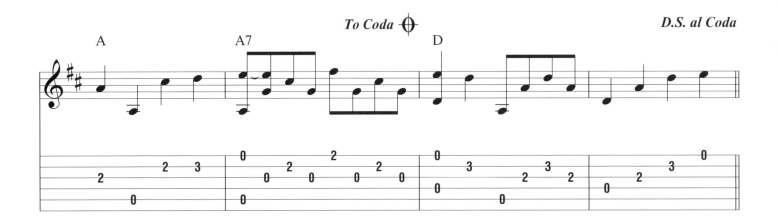

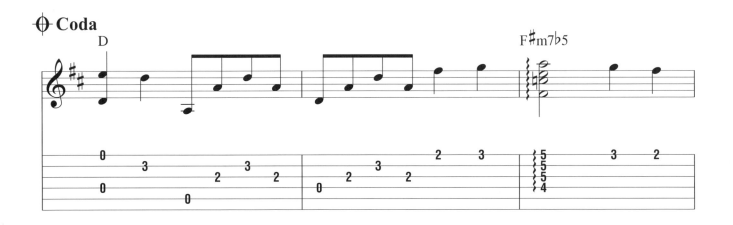

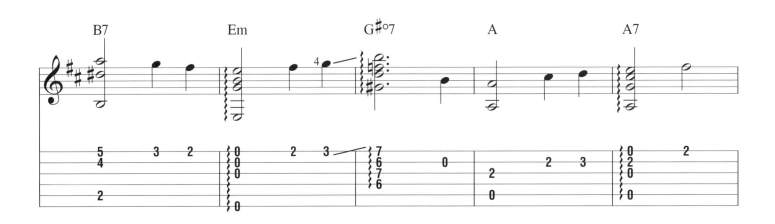

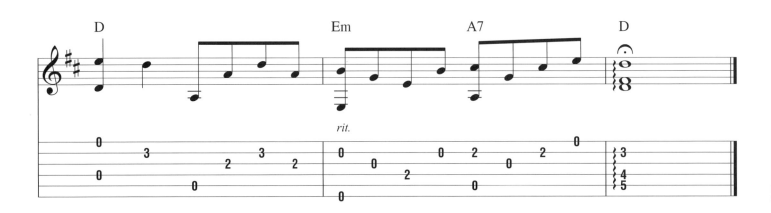

Christmas Time Is Here

from A CHARLIE BROWN CHRISTMAS

Words by Lee Mendelson
Music by Vince Guaraldi

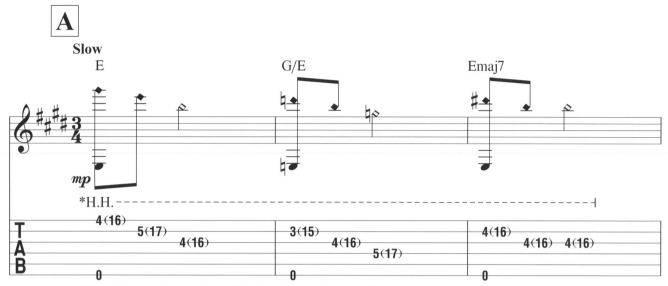

*Harp harmonics produced by lightly touching strings
12 frets above fretted notes while picking strings.

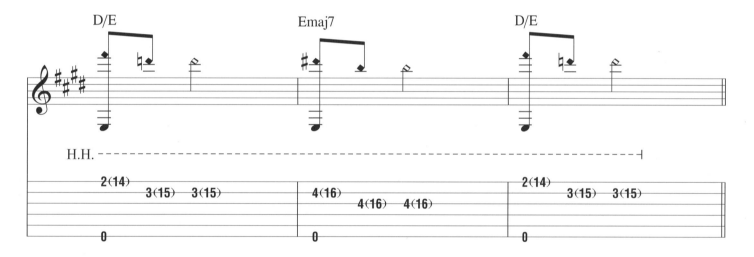

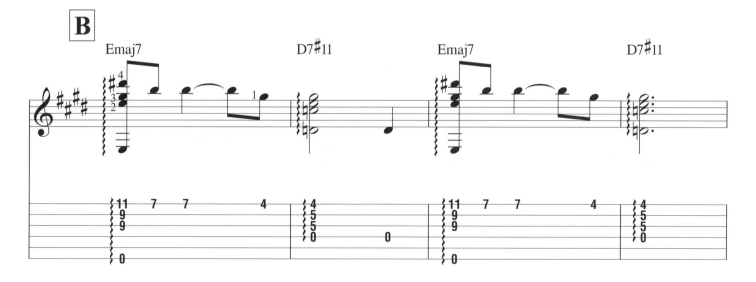

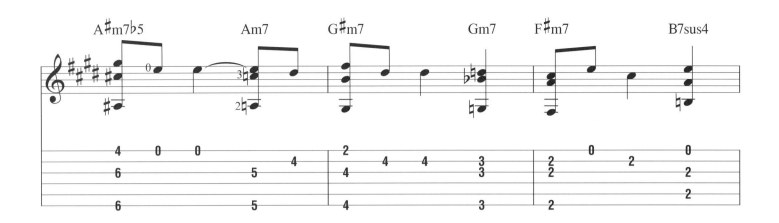

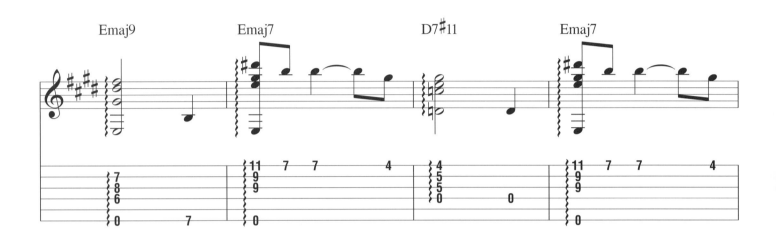

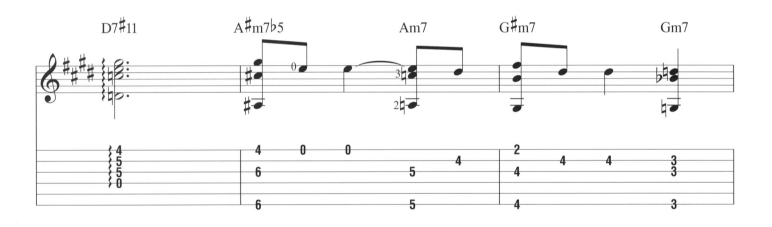

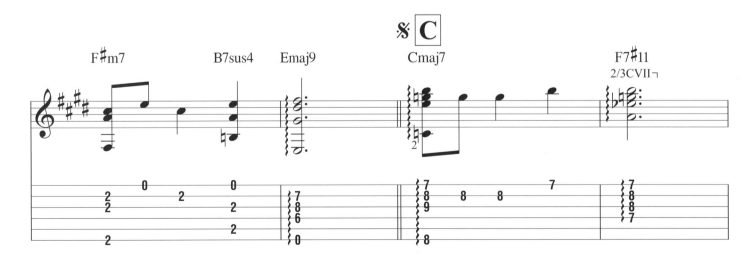

Happy Holiday

from the Motion Picture Irving Berlin's HOLIDAY INN
Words and Music by Irving Berlin

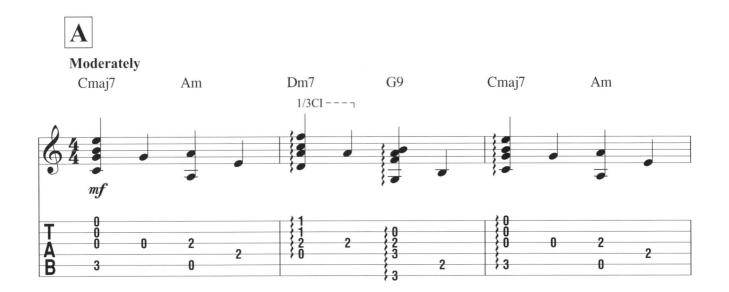

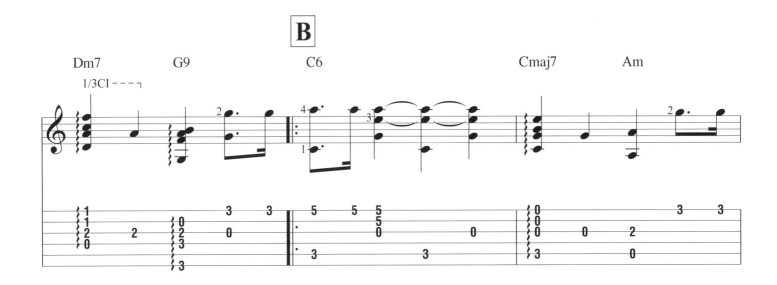

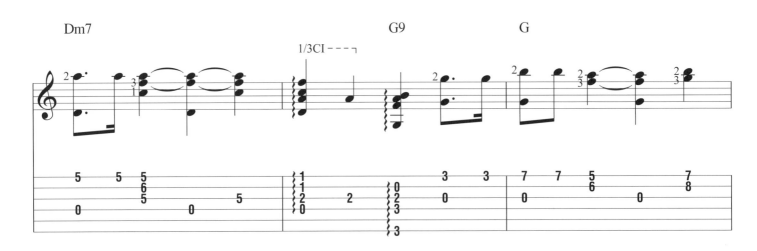

Happy Xmas
(War Is Over)

Written by John Lennon and Yoko Ono

Drop D tuning:
(low to high) D-A-D-G-B-E

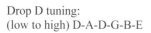

Slow

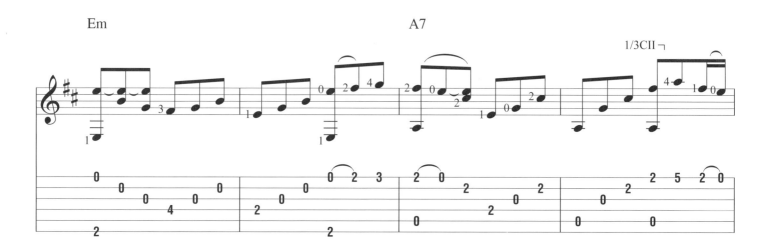

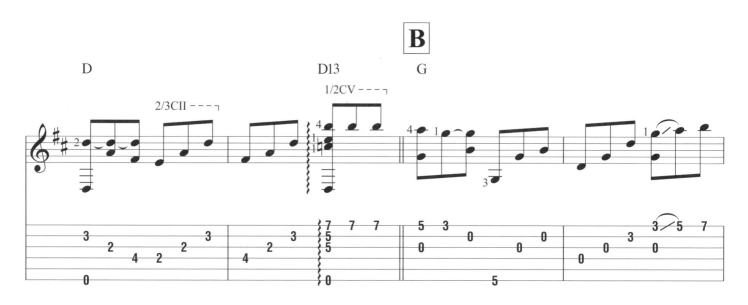

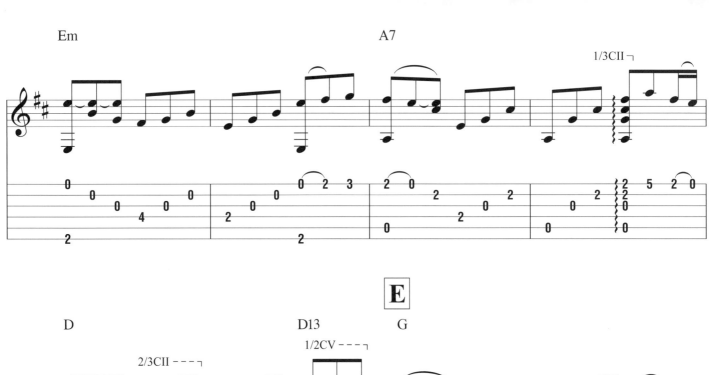

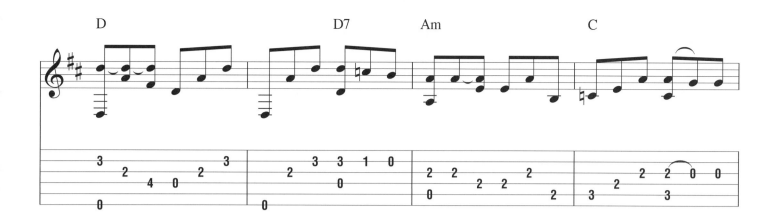

D.S. al Coda   ⊕ **Coda**

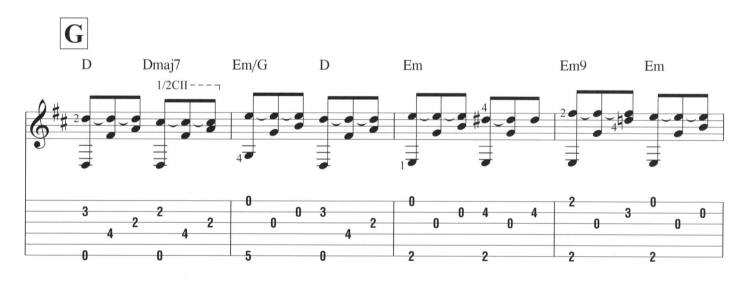

G

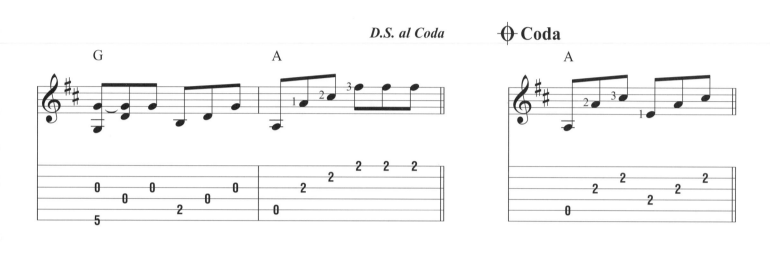

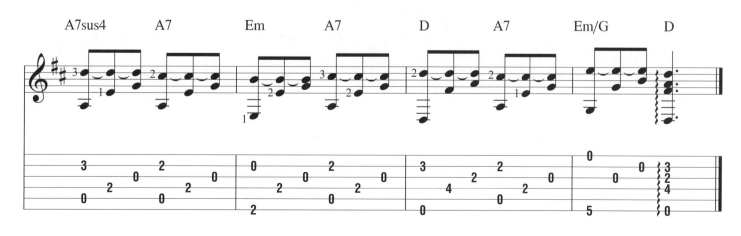

Have Yourself a Merry Little Christmas

from MEET ME IN ST. LOUIS

Words and Music by Hugh Martin and Ralph Blane

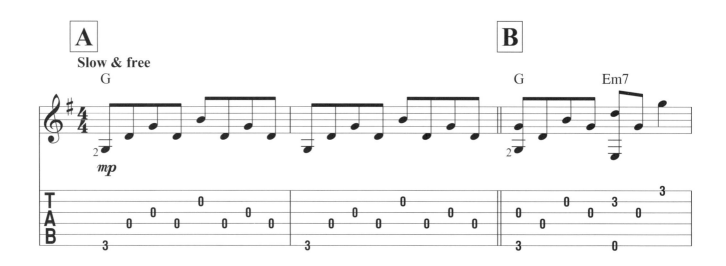

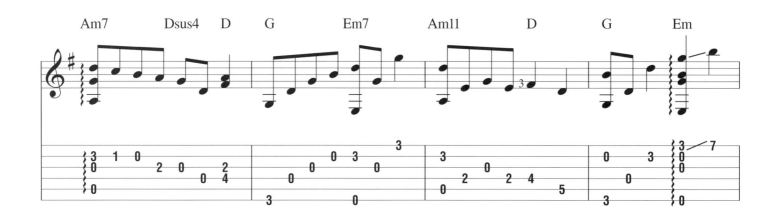

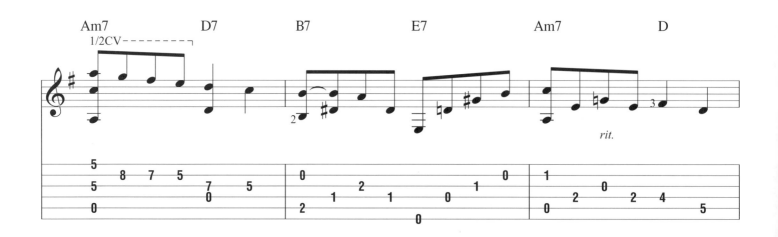

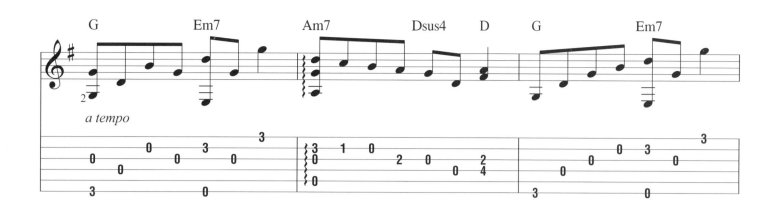

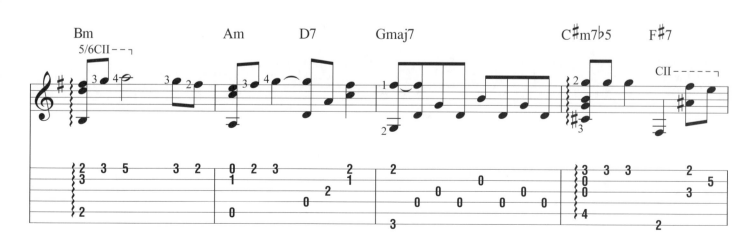

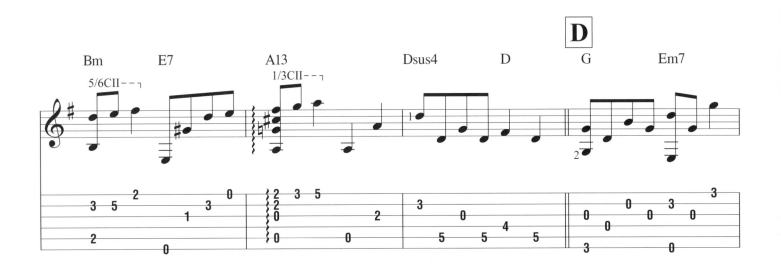

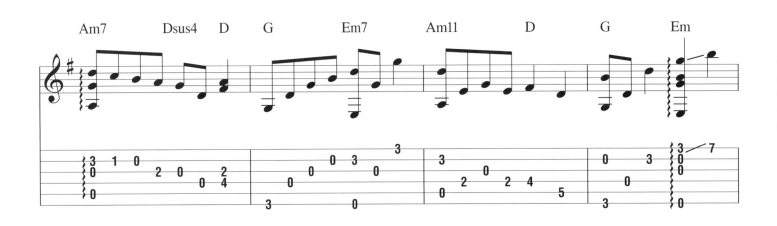

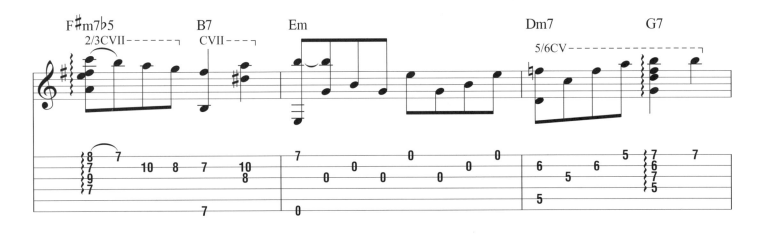

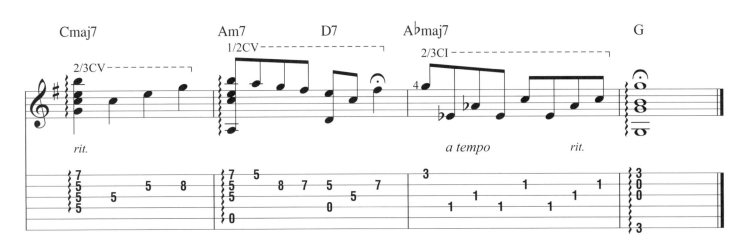

I'll Be Home for Christmas

Words and Music by Kim Gannon and Walter Kent

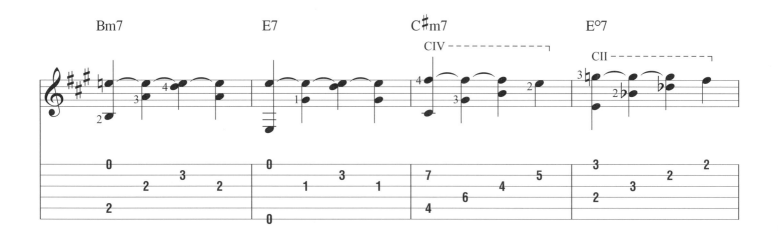

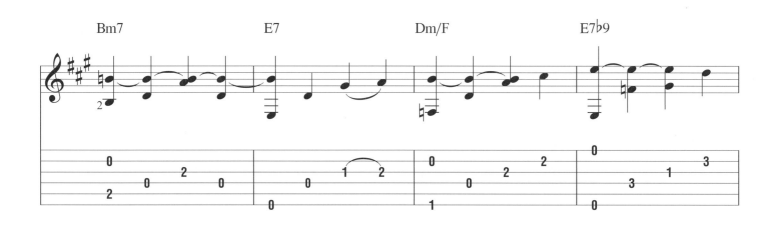

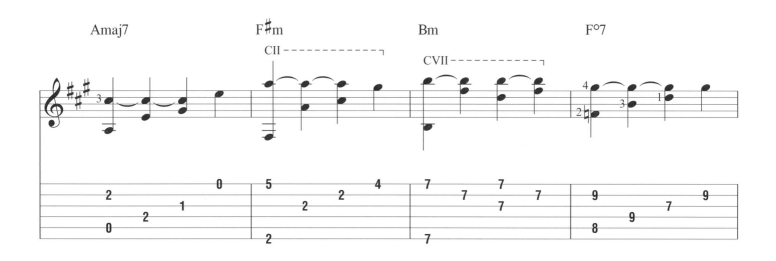

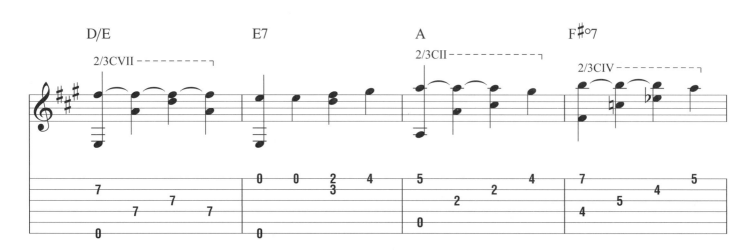

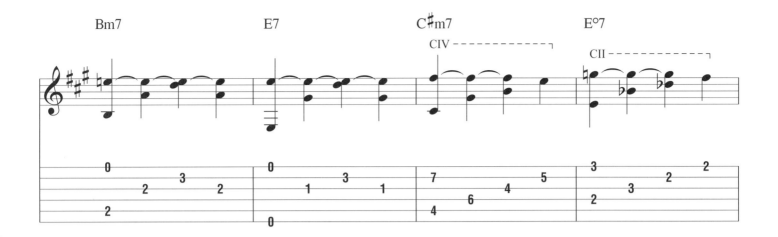

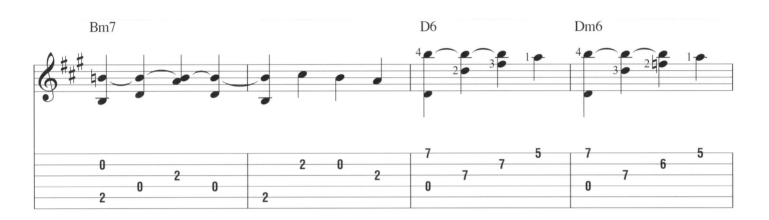

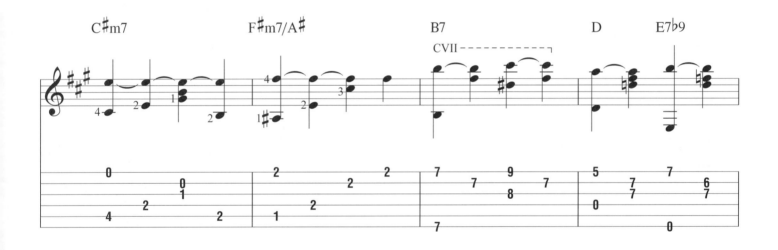

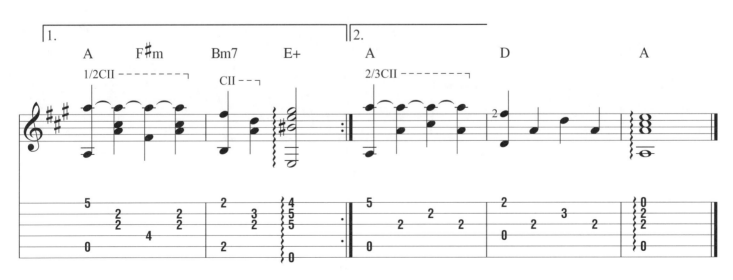

Let It Snow! Let It Snow! Let It Snow!

Words by Sammy Cahn
Music by Jule Styne

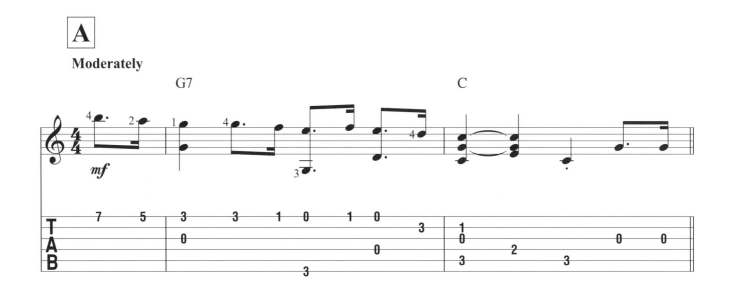

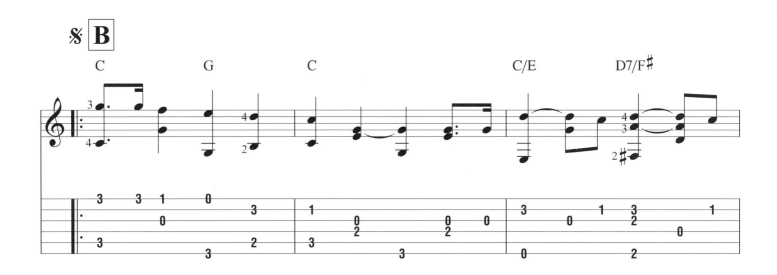

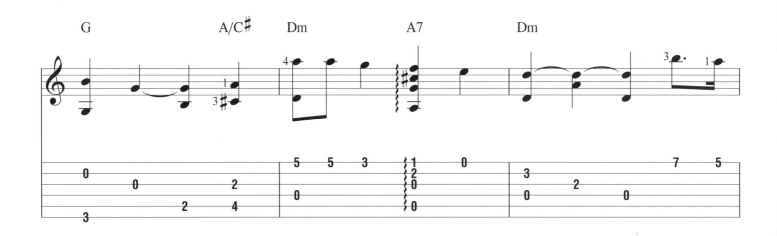

My Favorite Things

from THE SOUND OF MUSIC

Lyrics by Oscar Hammerstein II
Music by Richard Rodgers

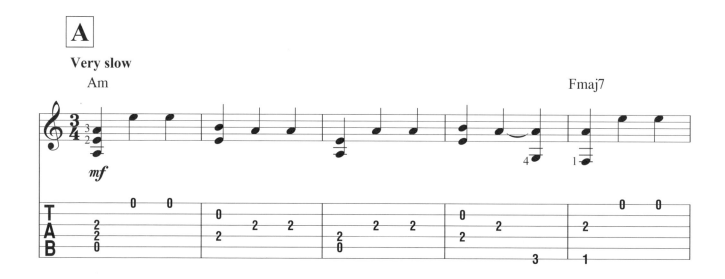

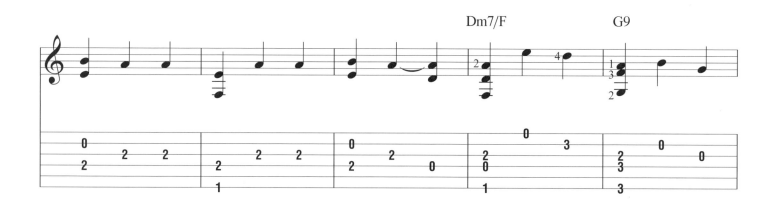

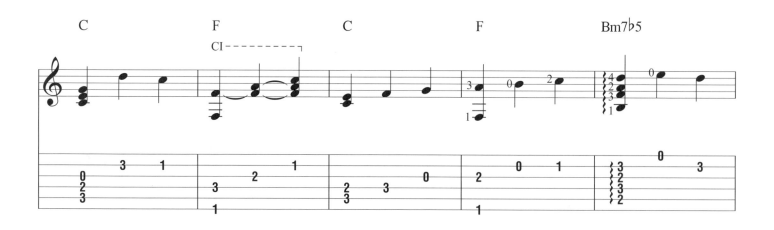

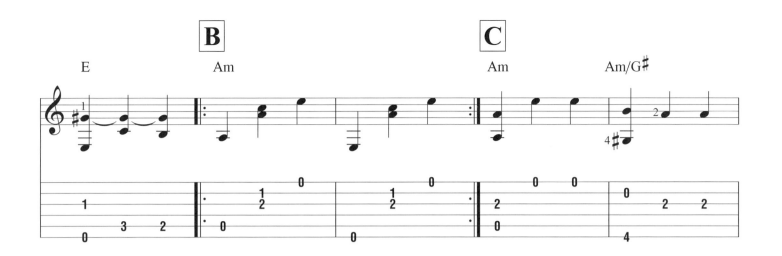

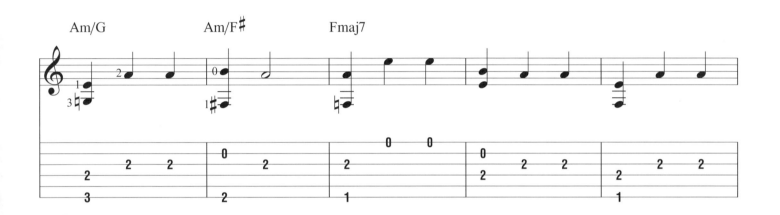

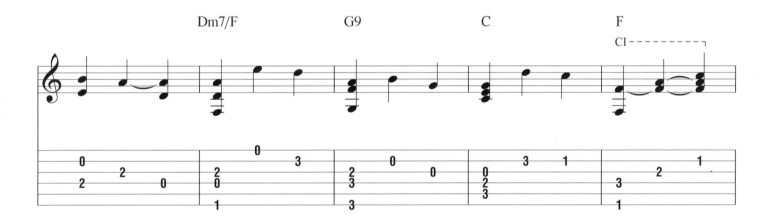

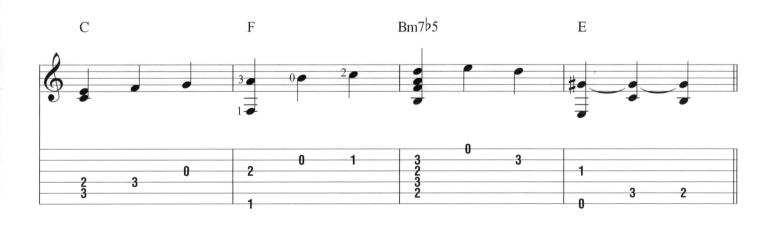

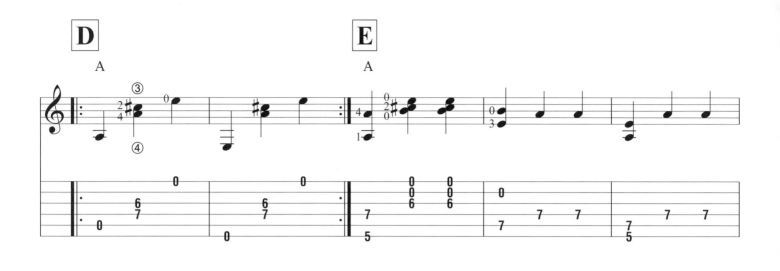

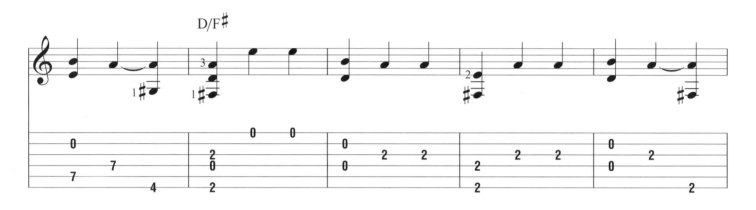

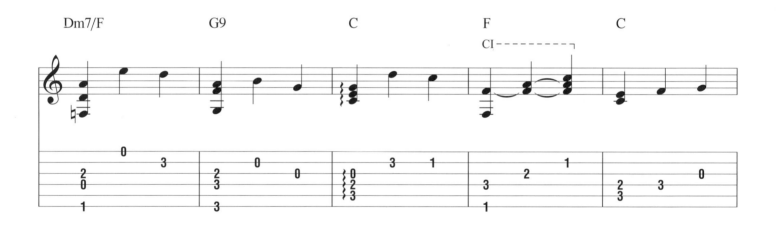

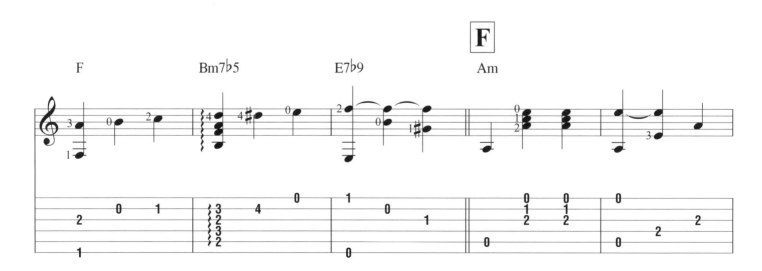

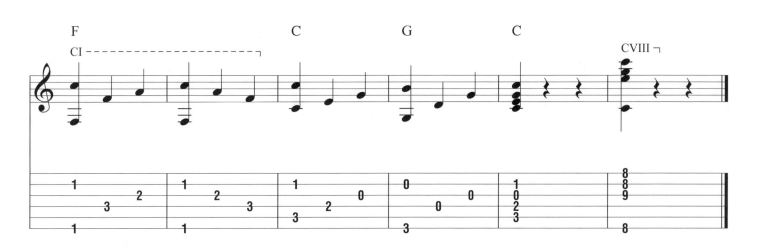

Santa Baby

By Joan Javits, Phil Springer and Tony Springer

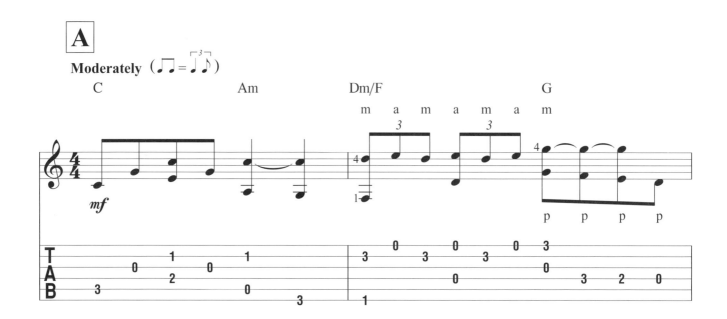

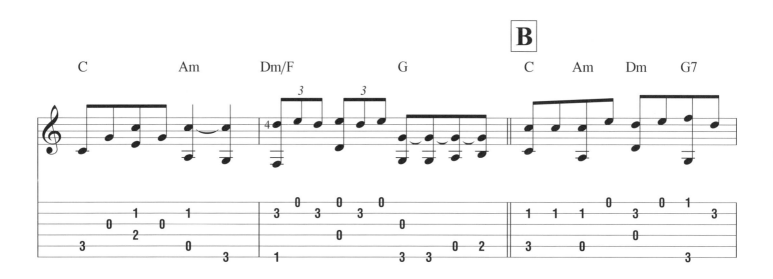

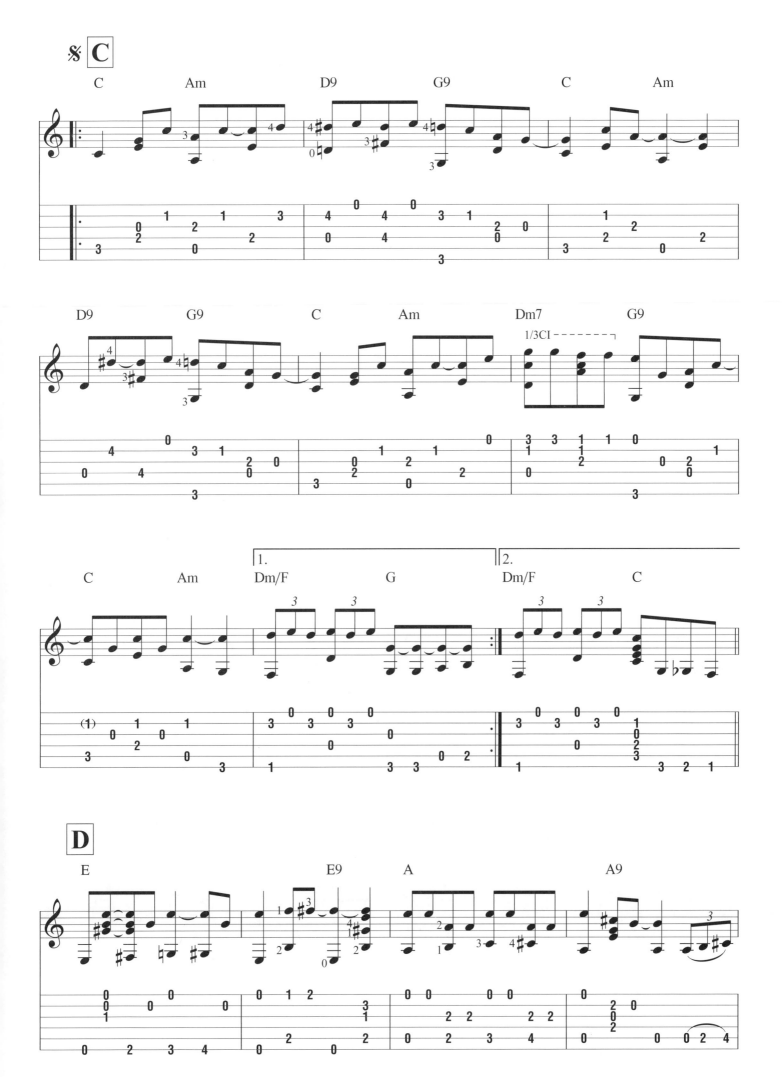

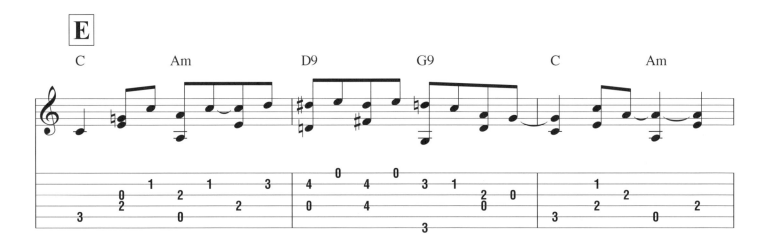

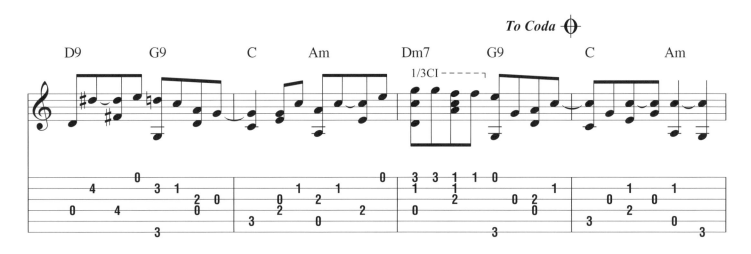

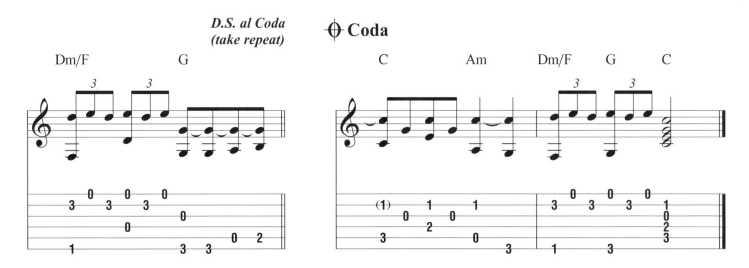

Silver and Gold

Music and Lyrics by Johnny Marks

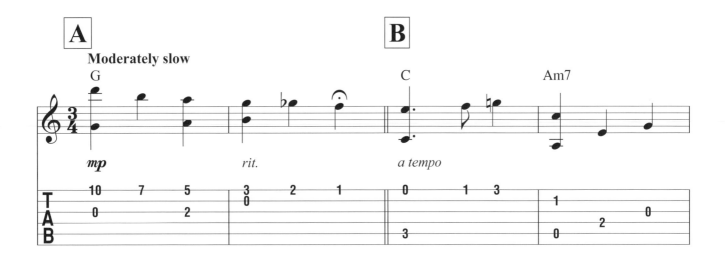

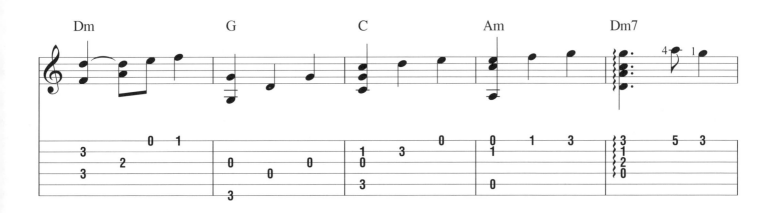

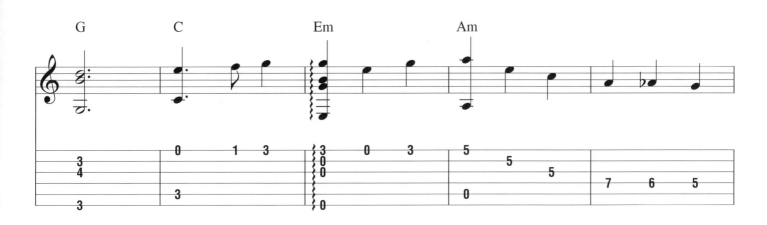

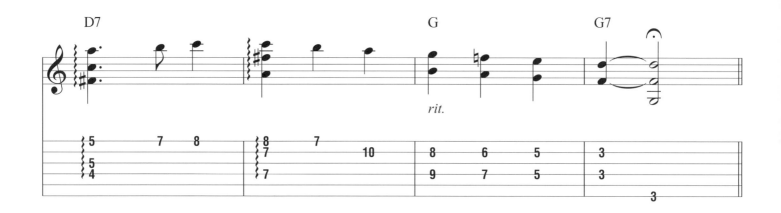

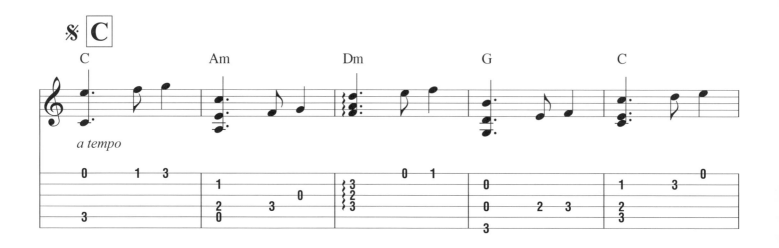

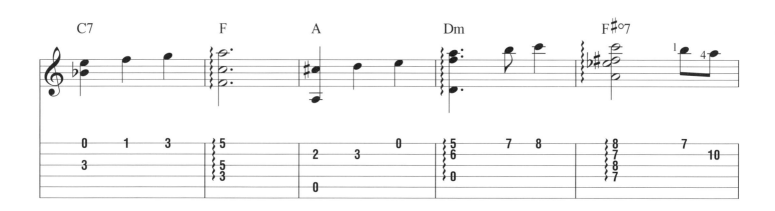

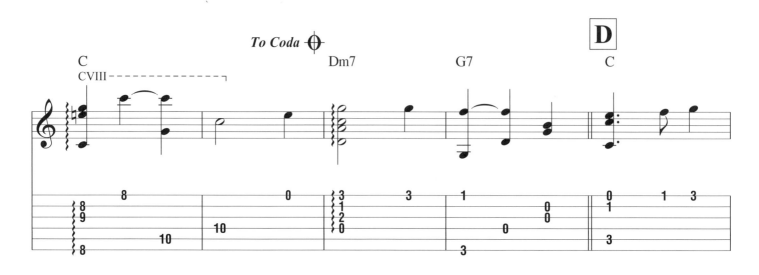

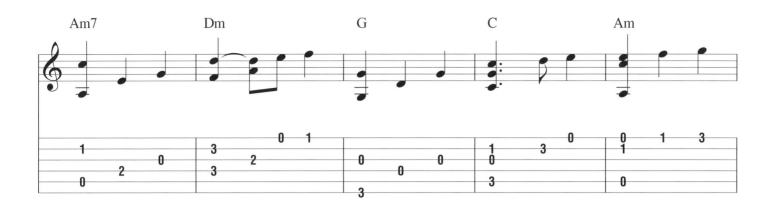

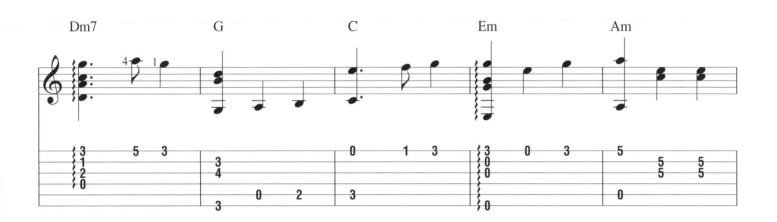

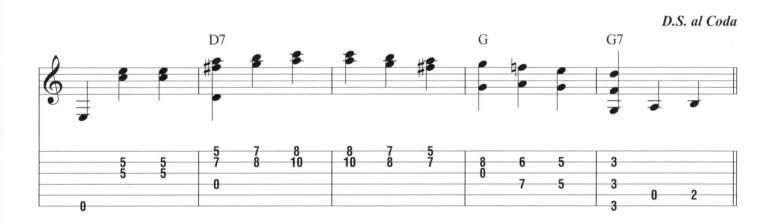

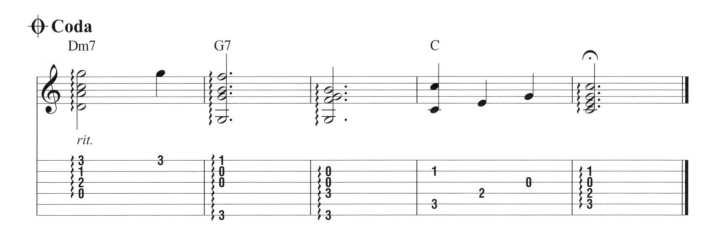

(There's No Place Like) Home for the Holidays

Words and Music by Al Stillman and Robert Allen

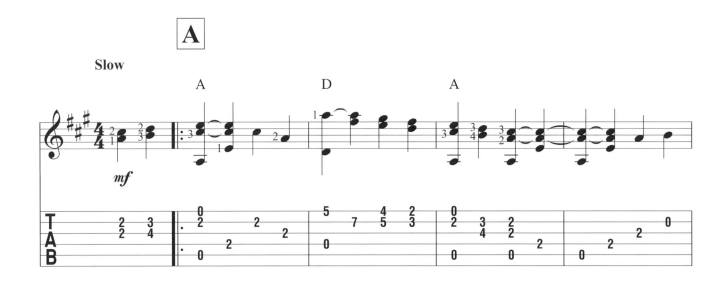

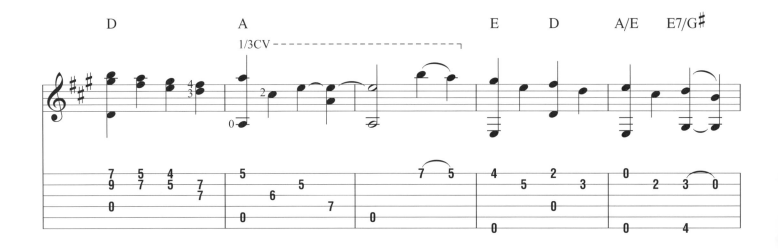

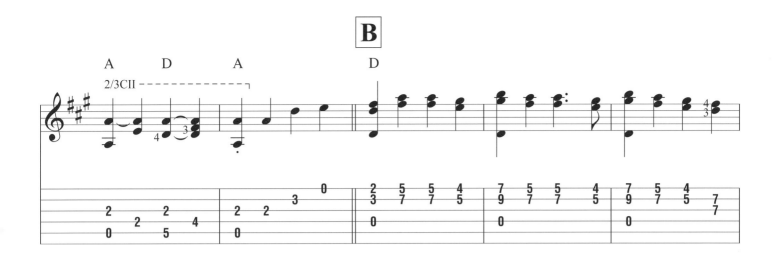

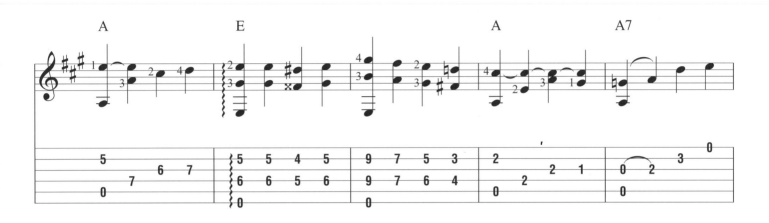

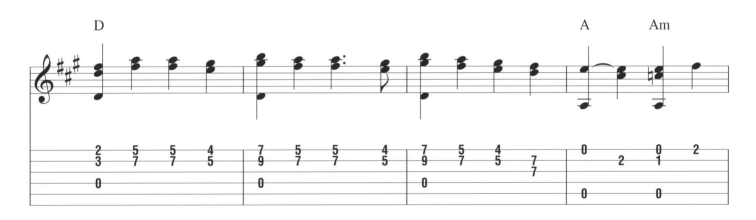

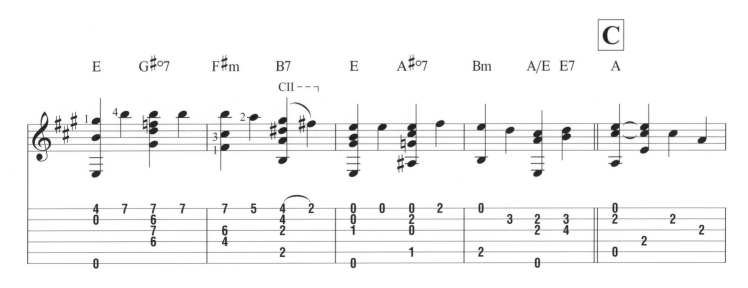

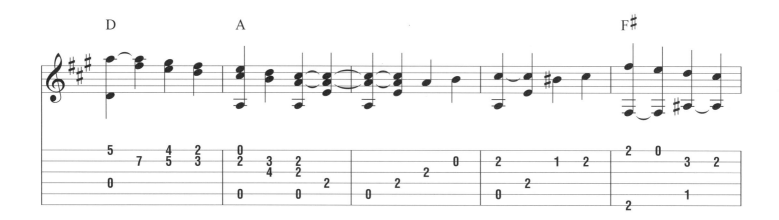

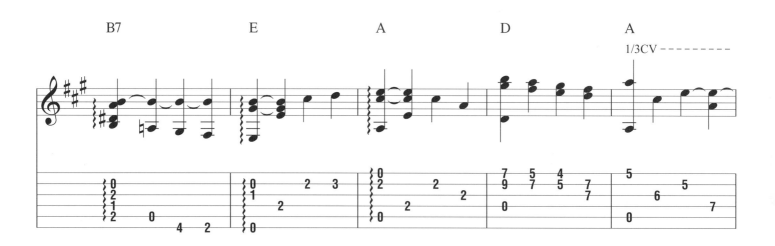

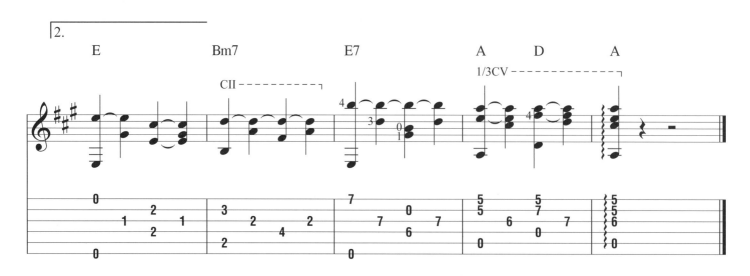

White Christmas

from the Motion Picture Irving Berlin's HOLIDAY INN

Words and Music by Irving Berlin

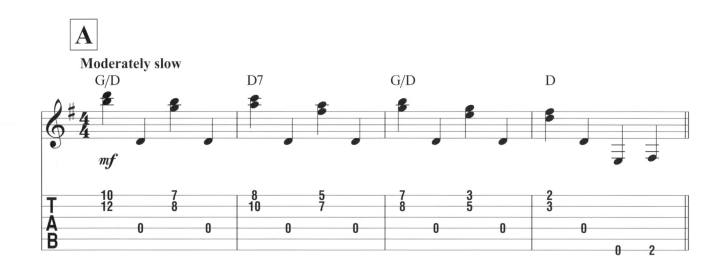

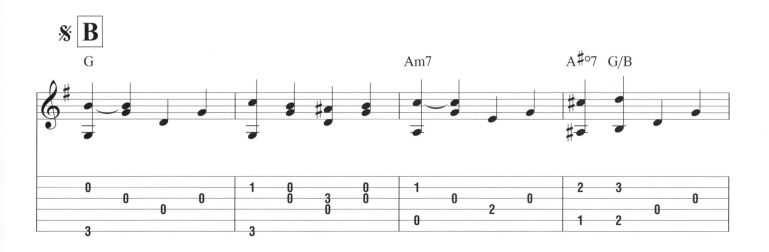

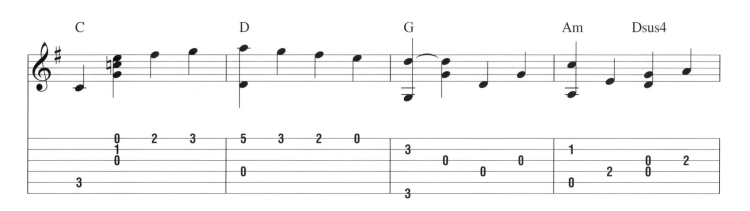

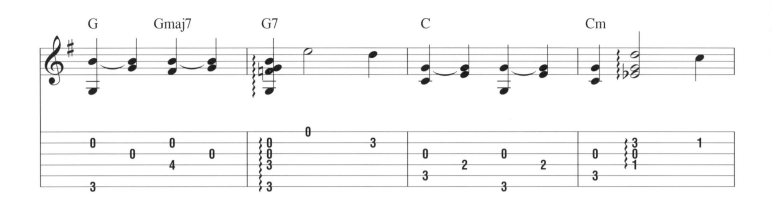

C

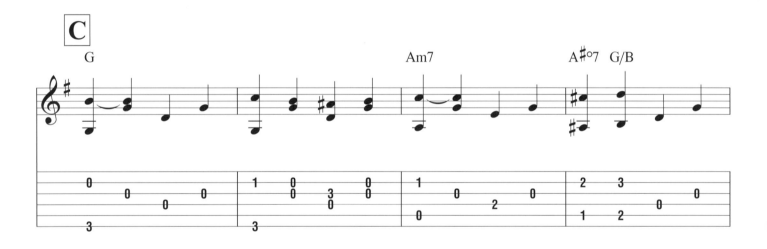

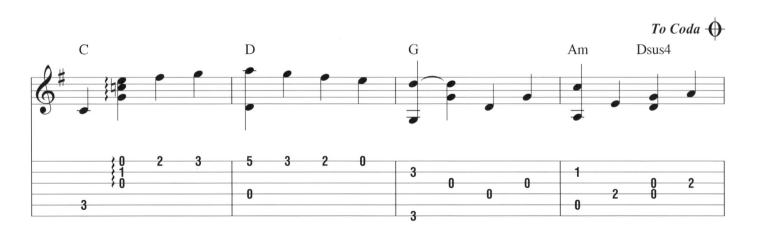

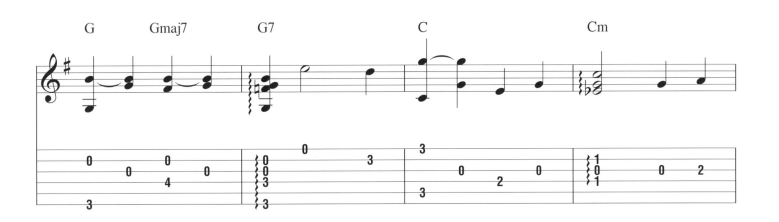

D.S. al Coda

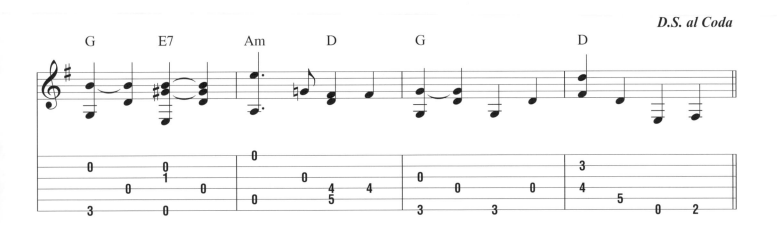

⊕ **Coda**

Slower

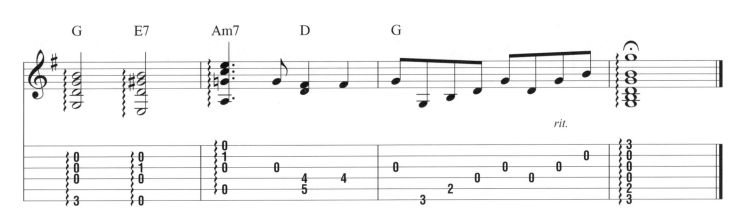

rit.

What Are You Doing New Year's Eve?

By Frank Loesser

Drop D tuning:
(low to high) D-A-D-G-B-E

Winter Wonderland

Words by Dick Smith
Music by Felix Bernard

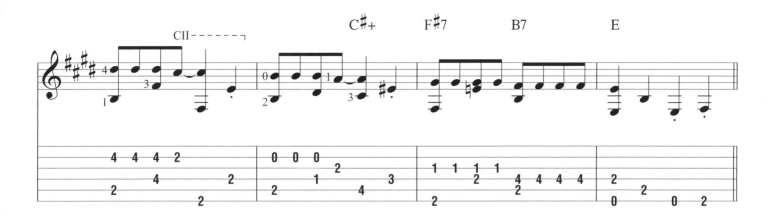

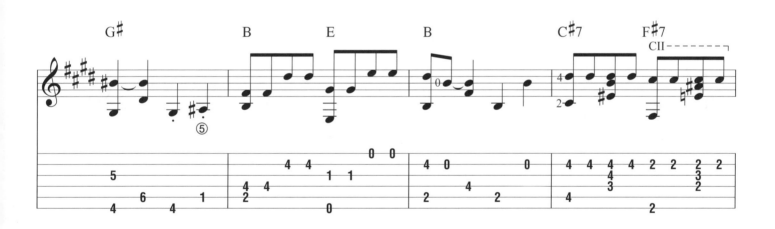

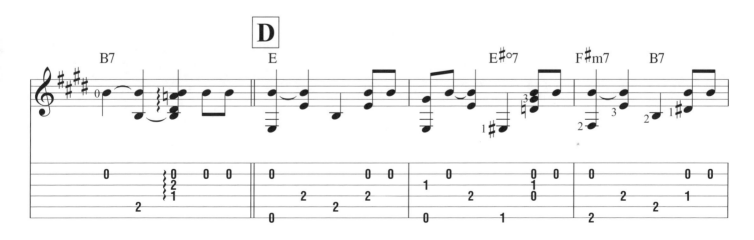

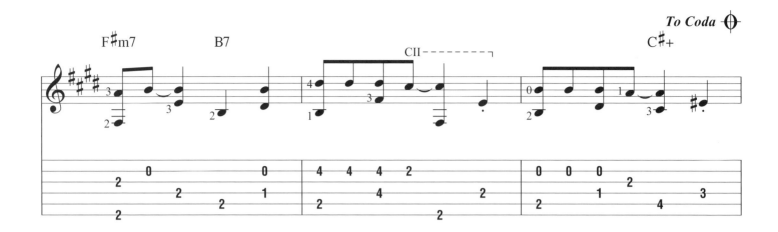

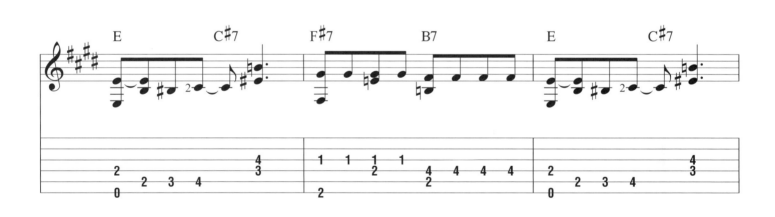

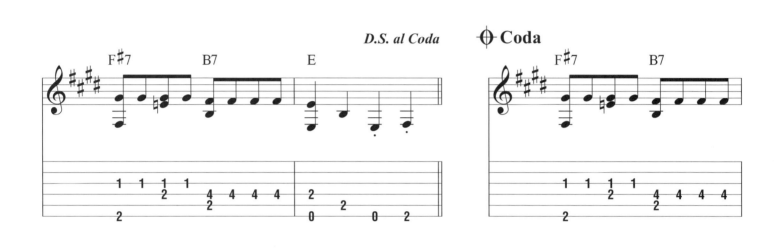

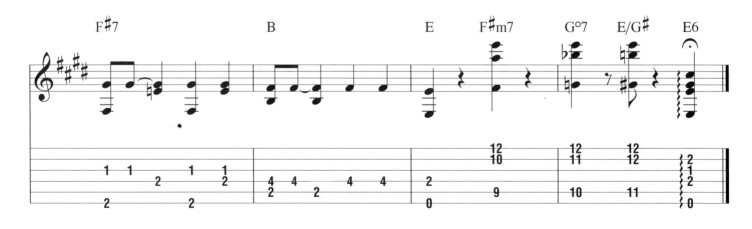